# First World War
and Army of Occupation
# War Diary
France, Belgium and Germany

9 DIVISION
2 Lowland Brigades
Royal Scots (Lothian Regiment)
5/6th Battalion.
1 March 1919 - 31 October 1919

WO95/1776/8

The Naval & Military Press Ltd
www.nmarchive.com
**Published in association with The National Archives**

Published by

## The Naval & Military Press Ltd

Unit 10 Ridgewood Industrial Park,

Uckfield, East Sussex,

TN22 5QE England

Tel: +44 (0) 1825 749494

www.naval-military-press.com

www.nmarchive.com

*This diary has been reprinted in facsimile from the original. Any imperfections are inevitably reproduced and the quality may fall short of modern type and cartographic standards.*

**© Crown Copyright**
**Images reproduced by permission of The National Archives, London, England, 2015.**

# Contents

| Document type | Place/Title | Date From | Date To |
|---|---|---|---|
| Heading | Highland (9) Division 2nd Lowland Bde 5/6 Bn Royal Scots 1919 Mar-1919 Oct From 32 Div 17 Bde | | |
| War Diary | Beuel | 01/03/1919 | 13/03/1919 |
| War Diary | Central-Grafrath | 14/03/1919 | 17/03/1919 |
| War Diary | Wald | 18/03/1919 | 27/04/1919 |
| War Diary | Ohligs | 28/04/1919 | 09/07/1919 |
| War Diary | Nettesheim | 10/07/1919 | 25/08/1919 |
| War Diary | Duren | 26/08/1919 | 31/10/1919 |

# HIGHLAND (9) DIVISION

## 2ND LOWLAND BDE

### 5/6 BN ROYAL SCOTS

1919 MAR – 1919 OCT

From 32 DIV 14 BDE

**WAR DIARY**
or
**INTELLIGENCE SUMMARY**
(Erase heading not required)

Army Form C. 2118.

5th Bn The Royal Scots

WO 33

| Place | Date | Hour | Summary of Events and Information | Remarks and references to Appendices |
|---|---|---|---|---|
| BEUEL | 1-3-19 | | Strength of Battalion 39 officers 574 O.Rs | A.F. |
| do | 2-3-19 | | Cleaning of Equipment. Inspection. 1 Coy on outpost duty | A.F. |
| do | 3-3-19 | | Church Parade. do | A.F. |
| do | 4-3-19 | | Route march. do | A.F. |
| do | 5-3-19 | | 2 Companies attend lecture at the Canal. 1 Coy on outpost duty | A.F. |
| do | 6-3-19 | | 1 Company on outpost duty. 1 Coy on outpost duty | A.F. |
| do | 7-3-19 | | Company training. 1 Coy on outpost duty | A.F. |
| do | 8-3-19 | | Company training. 1 Coy attend lecture at the Canal. 1 Coy on outpost duty | A.F. |
| do | 9-3-19 | | 2 Coys on Company training. 1 Coy on outpost duty | A.F. |
| do | 10-3-19 | | Cleaning of Equipment. Inspection. 1 Coy on outpost duty | A.F. |
| do | | | Church Parade. Outpost Coy relieved by 1/5th Kings Own Liverpool Regt. | |
| do | 11-3-19 | | Battalion Drill and Inspection by C.O. | A.F. |
| do | 12-3-19 | | Battalion was inspected by Major General L.J. Bolbert C.A. C.M.G. | A.F. |
| do | 13-3-19 | | On leaving the 32nd Division to join the Iceland (Cokes) Division of the Army of the Rhine the Battalion entrained at BEUEL leaving at 09:30 hrs arriving ORLIGS at 12:15 hrs and marched to Billets at CENTRAL and GRAFRATH. Lieut. S McAvoy MC, R.Q.M. Orrville, The R.S.Mann, J. Anstie, S.B. Sergt. J. Scott MM, L. Guile 2m/Room MM, L. Potterton & 115 O.Rs joined Batt. from 32nd Bn. | Assistant training of officers |
| CENTRAL–GRAFRATH | 14-3-19 | | Company training. | |

Army Form C. 2118.

1/16th Bn The Royal Scots

# WAR DIARY
## or
## INTELLIGENCE SUMMARY.
*(Erase heading not required.)*

Instructions regarding War Diaries and Intelligence Summaries are contained in F.S. Regs., Part II. and the Staff Manual respectively. Title pages will be prepared in manuscript.

| Place | Date | Hour | Summary of Events and Information | Remarks and references to Appendices |
|---|---|---|---|---|
| CENTRAL-GRAFRATH | 15-3-19 | | Company Training | A.F. |
| do | 16-3-19 | | Church Parade | A.F. |
| do | 17-3-19 | | Station reported to billets in WALD. Suits ordered to recognise 7/16 R.S. Bn. Moved from GRAFRATH with 124 ORs. joined the WALD 39 ORs joined Batt. | M.F. |
| WALD | 18-3-19 | | Company training & Inspection. 2 Platoons on outpost duty | A.F. |
| do | 19-3-19 | | "A" Coy moving front on outpost line. 3 Companies relation & Company training. 2 Platoons on outpost duty. The Burgomaster, 2 R.B. Coode & Gardisch found Battalion | F.F. R.F.R. |
| do | 20-3-19 | | do | A.F. R.F.R. |
| do | 21-3-19 | | "A" Coy do 1 Off. 9 ORs Battalion | A.F. R.F. |
| do | 22-3-19 | | "A" Coy do 2 Officers joined Battalion by Coy. Inspection 1 Battalion | F.F. R.F.R. |
| do | | | "A" Coy training. 3 coys on Company training. 2 Platoon on outpost duty. 7/16 R.S. Lieutenant M.M. & 28 OR. off Btn joined 8th +32 ORs | F.F. A.F.R. |
| do | 23-3-19 | | Church Parade. 2 Platoons on outpost duty | F.F. A.F. |
| do | 24-3-19 | | Company Training "A" Cy moving 10 ORs. joined Batt. | A.F. |
| do | 25-3-19 | | do do 2 do | A.F. |
| do | 26-3-19 | | do do 2 do | F.F. B.F. |
| do | 27-3-19 | | 3 Coys of Infantry Training. Bomb drill. Cpt Melton leaving '1 Cpt Kong outpost held at 7/6th Chenaux joined train 11 R.S. 7th Wt Hampshire joined 21 O.R. The 2/B ancy Coy Cm outpost. The Assoc Cpt Durnbridge | A.F. |
| do | 28-3-19 | | Two Coys Company Training 21 ORs joined the Batt. 7 OR ORs rejected also on strength | A.F. |

1/5th Bn The Royal Scots.

Army Form C. 2118.

## WAR DIARY
or
## INTELLIGENCE SUMMARY
(Erase heading not required.)

| Place | Date | Hour | Summary of Events and Information | Remarks and references to Appendices |
|---|---|---|---|---|
| WALD | 19-3-19 | | Lewis Gun training. Coy & Platoon training. 9 O.R. joined Bn. | |
| do | 20-3-19 | | School Parades. Capt. O'Rae, The Bl. Black proceeded 12.0.c. | |
| do | 21-3-19 | | "A" Company. 3 Coys & Lewis Gun Coy & Platoon training. arms drill. Strength of Battalion 64 officers 915 O.R. | |

J.A. Tracy Lieut Col Commanding
1/5 Bn The Royal Scots

# WAR DIARY

**Army Form C. 2118.**

5th Bn. The Royal Scots

## INTELLIGENCE SUMMARY
(Erase heading not required.)

| Place | Date | Hour | Summary of Events and Information | Remarks and references to Appendices |
|---|---|---|---|---|
| Said | 1.4.19 | | "D" Coy. Armd. wiring party for Outpost Line. Remainder of "D" Coy + "E" Coy carry out Specialist class. | |
| | 4.4.19 | | "D" Coy continues wiring. Remainder of Battn. carry out Training Programme | |
| | 5.4.19 | | 50 men from "D" Coy + 15 men who are available to demobilization proceeded (Advance party) of Battn. on leaving. | |
| | 6.4.19 | | Church Parade | |
| | | | "B" + "C" Coys move to Gujrat. "A" Coy take over Guard Duties + Coys go on Great Eastern training. A.C. Coys on Patls. Lt. Col. C. Moore takes over | |
| | 7.4.19 | | "B" + "D" Coys continued training. | |
| | 8.4.19 | | command of the Battalion. | |
| | | | A.C. Transport, "B" + "D" Coy Baths | |
| | 9.4.19 | | A + D Coys have a Musical Education. Captain Gunn, 2/Lieut. Charles McVitty | |
| | 10.4.19 | | leave for Demobilization. | |
| | 11.4.19 | | "B" + "C" Coys have a Medical inspection. Transport inspected by Lt. Col. & C. Moore. Leaning up + inspection and Minor Physical training. | |
| | 12.4.19 | | Church Parade | |
| | 12.4.19 | | "A" + "C" Coy continued training. Wiring continued on Outpost Line by hivy parties of Demob. Camps | |
| | 14.4.19 | | Transport, Pack Tpt + "A" Coy. Baths. | |
| | 15.4.19 | | "B" + "D" Coys training | |
| | 16.4.19 | | B + C Coys training | |
| | 17.4.19 | | Gang Coop Guard men were granted a sickness. L.A.Capt. F. Young M.C. from Battn. Join 2nd Batn. the Royal Scots | |

Army Form C. 2118.

# WAR DIARY
## or
## INTELLIGENCE SUMMARY
(Erase heading not required.)

56th Bn. The Royal Devs

| Place | Date | Hour | Summary of Events and Information | Remarks and references to Appendices |
|---|---|---|---|---|
| Usedi | 18.4.19 | | The Commanding Officer inspects Gates. Who turned out on our football ground. Church Parade. | |
| | 19.4.19 | | | |
| | 20.4.19 | | A party of "D" Coy employed running at Cullen's line. The two Coys on training continue their programme. | |
| | 21.4.19 | | Gutenberg Baths. "D" & "A" Coy. Coys. Game. May 1st. "A" & "B" 22 Football Match. Result 2-2. | |
| | 22.4.19 | | Coy Hall at Museum. "D" Coy remainder of the Bn. do the training and inspection. | |
| | 23.4.19 | | Bath inspected by Brig. Gen. Lock, C.M.G., D.S.O. on football ground 5 at 10.00 hours. | |
| | 24.4.19 | | Training continues for "B" & "C" Coys. "D" & "A" have musical inspection | |
| | 25.4.19 | | Lt. Col. Graves, D.S.O. transfer to 5/3 S.W.B. Change of inspection "C" Coy reliant from outpost duty by 6th K.O.S.B. | |
| | 26.4.19 | | Church Parade. Q.M. stores move to Oliigo. Bath. Play match of 6.26 | |
| Oliigo | 27.4.19 | | "A" Coy. Reach Royal Eng. & Pont. R.S.M. 4 guns. | |
| | 28.4.19 | | Bath. Coy. shift to Oliigo. Having issued at 10-20 hrs. avoir only 45 to parade on training programme. | |
| | 29.4.19 | | Parade for organization of Lads. Balroi. 20 men for Coy. on fatigue duty. | |
| | 30.4.19 | | Parade as for Training Programme & Educational Classes. Parade as for Training Programme & Educational Classes. | |

T.C. modi, Lt. Col.
Comdg. 5/4th. The Royal Sus 7

**Army Form C. 2118.**

**WAR DIARY**
or
**INTELLIGENCE SUMMARY.**
(Erase heading not required.)

5/6th Br. H. Royal Scots

| Place | Date | Hour | Summary of Events and Information | Remarks and references to Appendices |
|---|---|---|---|---|
| Ollezy | May 4th | 10 a.m. | B Coy on outlying pignet. till 16.00 hours remnants of C Coy. The Pignet being thrown in one & couple. The Roads leaving our area permissions to hold a "May Day" Labour Demonstration | |
| | | 2 pm | D Coy supply 30 men for wiring on Outpost Line Remainder of Bn on training | |
| | | 2.8 | B Coy and H Coy exchange Roles. Remainder of Batt. Outposts and cleaning up. Jas Pickard Lieut Gen Sinclair accepts by Brigade. Capt Browning I presented & present to supplant | |
| | | 4 h | Church Parade | |
| 5 | 5th | C of D Coys on General Training | |
| | 7 h | C of D Coys on General Training | |
| | | 2 / Lt. O. Brizzi & R. Boulle proves to Us to inspect. Lieut Browning. 2/Lt R. McMillan to Us to inspect | |
| | 9 h | Batt on Route March | |
| | 10 h | Cleaning up & Inspection. Officer & 2/m Royal Park at Hockey Result 3-1 | |
| | 11 h | Church Parade | |
| | 12 h | B Coy wiring C & D Coy Genl Training | |

Army Form C. 2118.

**WAR DIARY**
or
**INTELLIGENCE SUMMARY.**
(Erase heading not required.)

5/6th Bn. the Royal Scots

| Place | Date | Hour | Summary of Events and Information | Remarks and references to Appendices |
|---|---|---|---|---|
| Ohrdrup | May 13. | | A Coy schung L & D Coys. Officers attend lecture by Brig. Gen. on subject in Corps. | |
| | 14 | | C Coy move to Gemunh on account of chicken. Remainder of Bn. stand to. | |
| | | | Lt. R.O. Laurie & 2/Lt. W. Gellaut proceed to Y.O. for discharge. | |
| | 15 | | Bath. on Route March. Officers play N.C.Os. at football – Result 3–1. | |
| | 16 | | C & D Coys Special Training. | |
| | 17 | | D Coy return from Gemunh. Remainder of Bat. inspection & carrying up. | |
| | 18 | | Church Parade | |
| | 19 | | Obliging digest concurred alternately by C & D Coys for period of 4 days covering U.25 O Ro. | |
| | 20 | | C Coy go for sail on the Rhine. Major A. D. Eretou S.O. take over command of the Bn. from Lt. Col. J. L. Miche to Command Depot the | |
| | 21 | | C & D Coys Leave S.B. Ris. makolis by Lyle. Gen. N.C.O. OS & EO Coys. | |
| | 22 | | Bat. on Route March. | |
| | 23 | | Kit Inspections & carrying of Bdlots. All available men from A & B Coys on using | |

Army Form C. 2118.

3/6th Bn. The Royal Scots

# WAR DIARY
## or
## INTELLIGENCE SUMMARY.
*(Erase heading not required.)*

| Place | Date | Hour | Summary of Events and Information | Remarks and references to Appendices |
|---|---|---|---|---|
| Ollup | May 24 | | Lieut. Darar | |
| | 25 | | A.B. & D. Coys. have S.B.R. inspects by Lieut Col. R.C.O. Li. Col. O.C. Murra takes over Command of Bn. from Major Holderton. | |
| | 26 | | C. Coy. go for sail to Coldera | |
| | 27 | | O. Coy. move to Benrah on account of strikes. Remainder of Bn. stand to | |
| | 28 | | Baths. Capt. V. Young, 2/Lt. A. McIntyre, 2/Lt. Anderson and Cockle proceeds to rest for inspection. | |
| | 29 | | C. Coy. Training A.B. Education | |
| | 30 | | C. Coy. Training A.B. Education. C.O. & Lieut and Quarter inspects Batt. of Lieut. Lt. Patterson takes command C. Coy vice Capt. Young sick for Demol, | |
| | 31 | | Cleaning of Billets and Inspections. | |

T.C. Inder, Lt. Col.
Comm.g 5/6 Bn. The Royal Scots

5/6 Roy Scots
2nd you 7 Sec
Form D1

Army Form C. 2118.

# WAR DIARY
## or
## INTELLIGENCE SUMMARY.
(Erase heading not required.)

Instructions regarding War Diaries and Intelligence Summaries are contained in F. S. Regs., Part II. and the Staff Manual respectively. Title pages will be prepared in manuscript.

| Place | Date | Hour | Summary of Events and Information | Remarks and references to Appendices |
|---|---|---|---|---|
| OHLIGS. | 1-6-19. | | Voluntary Church Parade. | |
| | 2-6-19. | | General Sir. William Robertson, inspects the Battalion. The following is an extract of letter received :-" The G.O.C. in Chief, The British Army of the Rhine wishes to convey to you, to Lieut. Colonel. T.C.Mudie and all ranks of the 5/6th. Bn. The Royal Scots his satisfaction at the turn out of the battalion and the smartness and steadiness of the men on parade. In particular he wishes to express his satisfaction of the turn out of the Battalion Transport". | |
| | 3-6-19. | | Being the King's Birthday the Battalion have a Colour Parade at 09.00 hoursand the remainder of the day observed as a holiday. Lt. Col. T.C.Mudie awarded the D.S.O. Major H.D.Carlton, D.S.O. gazetted Brevet Lt. Col. for distinguished service. | |
| | 4-6-19. | | "A" company fire at on 30 yards Range. | |
| | 5-6-19. | | Lewis Gun and Signalling Classes. B,C & D. companies carry out Musketry Training with the exception of those on Education. No. 15 Platoon accept "B" Coy's challenge at Football. Result:- B coy. 3   15 Platoon 0. | |
| | 6-6-19. | | "A" company commence firing at Brigade Range. "B" company commence firing on 30 yards Range. | |
| | 7-6-19. | | Battalion H.Qrs. company including start Education. "A" company continue firing at Brigade Range. | |

Army Form C. 2118.

# WAR DIARY
## or
## INTELLIGENCE SUMMARY.
*(Erase heading not required.)*

Instructions regarding War Diaries and Intelligence Summaries are contained in F. S. Regs., Part II. and the Staff Manual respectively. Title pages will be prepared in manuscript.

| Place | Date | Hour | Summary of Events and Information | Remarks and references to Appendices |
|---|---|---|---|---|
| OHLIGS. | 7-6-19. | | Lt. T.M.Barclay takes over command of "C" Company vice. Lt. G.W.M.Paterson. | |
| | 8-6-19. | | Church Parade. | |
| | 9-6-19. | | A & D. Companies Education. Lewis Gun and Signalling classes continue. Officers attend Lecture by Commanding Officer at 18.00 hours. Subject- "Map Reading". | |
| | 10-6-19. | | Battalion have a holiday. "D" company have a "Sports Day". | |
| | 11-6-19. | | Lewis Gun, Signalling and Musketry classes. A & D. Companies attend Educational Classes. | |
| | 12-6-19. | | "A" company continue Range Practises. Remainder of battalion cleaning billets. | |
| | 13-6-19. | | "A" company continue Firing. Batt. H.Qrs. including Bands and remainder of B.C & D companies not on Education attend Lecture on "China and the Chinese" by Mr. Lawrence Derrick. | |
| | 14-6-19. | | Cleaning up and inspections. | |
| | 15-6-19. | | Church Parade. | |
| | 16-6-19. | | A & B. companies continue Firing. C & D companies on fatigues. | |
| | 17-6-19. | | A & B companies go on Rhine Trip- " Bonn to Coblenz" C & D companies on fatigues. | |
| | 18-6-19. | | "D" company supply Guards for Railway Bridges as a precaution against Bosche Intrigues. | |
| | 19-6-19. | | Battalion store all surplus kit etc., in Brigade Dump and prepare to move forward at short notice. | |

Army Form C. 2118.

# WAR DIARY
## or
## INTELLIGENCE SUMMARY
(Erase heading not required.)

Instructions regarding War Diaries and Intelligence Summaries are contained in F. S. Regs., Part II. and the Staff Manual respectively. Title pages will be prepared in manuscript.

| Place | Date | Hour | Summary of Events and Information | Remarks and references to Appendices |
|---|---|---|---|---|
| OHLIGS. | 20-6-19. | | "A" company on Education. Probationers Signalling Class of 6 men per company commences. | |
| | 21-6-19. | | Battalion parade at 14.00 hours for Baths at WALD. | |
| | 22-6-19. | | Cleaning up and inspections. Sports Meeting held in afternoon. | |
| | 23-6-19. | | Church Parade. | |
| | 23-6-19. | | Battalion prepare to move forward should the Bosche not sign the Peace Terms and at 19.00 hours all companies report that they are ready to move at a moments notice. 20.15 hours orders received to stand down. | |
| | 24-6-19. | | Re-organisation, issuing of Blankets and Spare Clothing. | |
| | 25-6-19. | | "A" company fire practice at Brigade Range. "B" company on Training. C & D. on duties. Probationers signalling classes. | |
| | 26-6-19. | | "A" company continue firing. "B" company fire on 30 yards Range. Battalion parade in afternoon for swimming baths. | |
| | 27-6-19. | | A company complete Range Practice. "B" coy. firingxxxx Training. | |
| | 28-6-19. | | Cleaning up and inspections. | |
| | 29-6-19. | | Church Parade. | |
| | 30-6-19. | | "A" coy. Training. "B" coy. Education. C & D companies Duties. | |

A B Carlow Lt Col
Comdg 1/6 the Royal Scots

Army Form C. 2118.

# WAR DIARY 5/6th Bn. The Royal Scots.
## or
## INTELLIGENCE SUMMARY.
*(Erase heading not required.)*

Instructions regarding War Diaries and Intelligence
Summaries are contained in F. S. Regs., Part II.
and the Staff Manual respectively. Title pages
will be prepared in manuscript.

| Place | Date JULY, 1919. | Hour | Summary of Events and Information | Remarks and references to Appendices |
|---|---|---|---|---|
| Ohligs. | 1. | | "A" Coy. Training, "B" & "C" Coys. Education. "D" Coy. Duties. | |
| | 2. | | "A" Coy. Education, "B" Coy. Firing on Brigade Range, "C" & "D" Coys. Duties. In the Afternoon, Battalion Parade for Baths. | |
| | 3. | | Companies at disposal of Company Commanders. | |
| | 4. | | Observed as a holiday. | |
| | 5. | | Cleaning of Billets and Kit Inspections. | |
| | 6. | | Special Thanksgiving Service. | |
| | 7. | | Companies at disposal of Company Commanders. | |
| | 8. | | "C" & "D" Coys. Duties. "A" & "B" Baths. | |
| | 9. | | Battalion Parade at 07.20 hours and entrain at OHLIGS Station. Battalion reach their new Billeting Area at 13.30 hours. | |
| Nettesheim. | 10. | | Coys. at disposal of Coy. Commanders for organization of their new billets. "D" Coy. billeted in ROMMERSKIRCHEN, "A", "B" and H.Q. in NETTESHEIM, and "C" Coy. in ANSTEL. | |
| | 11. | | Coys. at disposal of Company Commanders. | |
| | 12. | | Cleaning of Billets and Kit Inspection. | |
| | 13. | | Church Parade. | |

Army Form C. 2118.

# WAR DIARY 5/6th Bn. The Royal Scots.
## or
## INTELLIGENCE SUMMARY.
*(Erase heading not required.)*

Instructions regarding War Diaries and Intelligence Summaries are contained in F. S. Regs., Part II. and the Staff Manual respectively. Title pages will be prepared in manuscript.

| Place | Date | Hour | Summary of Events and Information | Remarks and references to Appendices |
|---|---|---|---|---|
| | JULY, 1919. | | | |
| Nettesheim. | 14. | | "A" & "D" Coys. Education, "B" & "C" Coys. Training, Probationary Signalling Class of six men per Company, re-commences. | |
| | 15. | | "A", "C" and "D" Coys. Training, "B" Coy. Education. | |
| | 16. | | "A", "B" and "C" Coys. Training, "D" Coy. Education. | |
| | 17. | | "A", "B" and "D" Coys. Company Training. "C" Company Baths. | |
| | 18. | | Cross Country Run by Companies. | |
| | 19. | | General Holiday, National rejoicing for Peace. | |
| | 20. | | Church Parades. | |
| | 21. | | "A" & "D" Coys. Education, "C" Coy. Coy. Training, "B" Coy. Range Practice. | |
| | 22. | | "A" Coy. Company Training, "B" & "C" Education, "D" Range Practice. Scouts Class assembles. | |
| | 23. | | Lecture on War Savings Certificates by a Rhine Army Lecturer. Company Training and Education. | |
| | 24. | | "B" & "C" Coys. Education. "A" & "D" Coys. Company Training. | |
| | 25. | | Cross Country Run. | |
| | 26. | | Cleaning of Billets and Kit Inspection. | |
| | 27. | | Church Parades. | |
| | 28. | | "A" & "D" Coys. Education, "B" & "C" Coys. Company Training. | |

Army Form C. 2118.

# WAR DIARY 5/6th Bn. The Royal Scots.
## *or*
## INTELLIGENCE SUMMARY.
(*Erase heading not required.*)

Instructions regarding War Diaries and Intelligence Summaries are contained in F. S. Regs., Part II. and the Staff Manual respectively. Title pages will be prepared in manuscript.

| Place | Date JULY, 1919. | Hour | Summary of Events and Information | Remarks and references to Appendices |
|---|---|---|---|---|
| Nettesheim. | 29. | | "A" & "D" Coys. Company Training, "B" & "C" Coys. Education. | |
| | 30. | | Battalion Sports and Concert in Evening by the Battalion Troupe, "CHEERIOS". Company Training & Educ. | |
| | 31. | | Battalion Cross Country Run. Winning Company "C" Coy. | |
| | 1-8-19. | | Lieut. Colonel,<br>Commanding, 5/6th Battalion The Royal Scots. | |

Army Form C. 2118.

32585    20/10/19
5/1b Royal Scots

# WAR DIARY
## or
## INTELLIGENCE SUMMARY.
*(Erase heading not required.)*

Instructions regarding War Diaries and Intelligence Summaries are contained in F. S. Regs., Part II. and the Staff Manual respectively. Title pages will be prepared in manuscript.

| Place | Date | Hour | Summary of Events and Information | Remarks and references to Appendices |
|---|---|---|---|---|
| Fettesheim | August. | | | |
| | 1st. | | Battalion Cross Country Run. Winning Company, "G" Coy. | |
| | 2nd | | Lecture by Rev. G.V. HASLETT, B.A. on Venereal Disease. | |
| | 3rd | | Church Parades. Cricket Match. H.Q. versus "C" Coy. | |
| | 4th | | General Holiday (Bank Holiday) 1 limber, 1 cooker and 1 water cart in Cavalry Corps Horse Show. | COLOGNE. |
| | 5th | | "A" and "D" Coys. Baths. "B" and "C" Coys. Education. | |
| | 6th | | "A" and "B" Coys. Education. "B" Coy. Coy. Training. "C" Coy. Range Practices. | |
| | 7th | | Cross Country Run. Lt.Col. C. Ludie, M.S.O. resumes command of the Bn. as from 4-6-19. | |
| | 8th | | Coys. at disposal of Coy. Commanders. | |
| | 9th | | Divine Services. | |
| | 10th | | "A" and "D" Coys - Education. "B" and "C" Coys - Coy. Training. | |
| | 11th | | "B" and "C" " " . Baths for Bn. Bn. Cricket Match with 8th Bn. R.G. Corps | |
| | 12th | | "A" and "D" Coys " " . "B" and "C" Education. Bn. will move to DUREN on 15th by bus. | |
| | 13th | | Coys. at disposal of Coy. Commanders for preparation for move. All specialist classes will cease until further orders. | |
| | 14th | | IV Corps Torchlight Tattoo at WIDDERN. Massed Pipers and Drummers now at WIDDERN, will play at Army Horse Show on 14th and 15th inst. | |
| | 15th | | The Battalion moved by bus to WIDDERN. | |
| | 16th | | Coys. at disposal of Coy. Commanders for re-organisation and cleaning up of quarters. | |
| | 17th | | Divine Service. | |
| | 18th | | Rhine trip for Battalion. | |
| | 19th | | Coys. at disposal of Coy. Commanders for cleaning up and preparation for Bde. Commander's inspection. | |
| | 20th | | Brigade Commander's Inspection of the Bn. H.Q., "A" and B Coys. on barrack square, E.S.M.O. "C and D Coys. Att. in barrack rooms. Transport "hooked in" and drawn up in rear of Battalion. "A" Coy. and B H.Q. Parade on Square at 10.00 hrs. for inspection by Adjutant, E.S.M.O. | |
| | 21st. | | "B" and "C" Coys. at disposal of Coy. Commanders. Divisional Commander inspects barracks. | |
| | 22nd. | | Bn. Route March. Capt. Murro will inspect catering on 22nd and 23rd inst. | |
| | | | Helmets and Packs. Capt. Murro will inspect catering on Band and 23rd inst. | |
| | 23rd | | Coys. at disposal of Coy. Commanders for inspection of Rifles, P.T. and Ceremonial Drill. | |
| | 24th | | Divine Service. | |
| | 25th | | "A" and "D" Coys. - Education. "C" and "B" Coys - Coy. Training, P.T. and Ceremonial Drill. Baths for "A" "B" and H.Q. in the afternoon. | |

Army Form C. 2118.

# WAR DIARY
## or
## INTELLIGENCE SUMMARY.
*(Erase heading not required.)*

Instructions regarding War Diaries and Intelligence Summaries are contained in F. S. Regs., Part II. and the Staff Manual respectively. Title pages will be prepared in manuscript.

| Place | Date | Hour | Summary of Events and Information | Remarks and references to Appendices |
|---|---|---|---|---|
| DURBER. | August. 26th | | "B" and "C" Coys. - Coy. Training. P.T. and Ceremonial Drill. Baths for "C" and "D" and transport in afternoon. "CHUMPS" Concert Party will give a concert in Theatre at 18.00 hours. | |
| | 27th. | | "C" and "D" Coys. - Education. "B" and "C" Coys. Coy. Training, P.T. and Ceremonial Drill | |
| | 28th. | | "B" and "C" Coys. " " "A" and "D" " " " " " | |
| | 29th. | | "B" and "C" Coys. " " | |
| | | | Bn. Route March. Parade on Square at 09.00 hours. Tank Corps Sports on "Bavaria Sports Ground" at 14.30 hours. | |
| | 30th. | | 08.30 - 10.00 hrs. Interior Economy. 10.30 Bn. will Parade on Square for Memorial Drill. The Battalion will probably move to the U.K. between the 23rd and 28th September. | |
| | 31st. | | Divine Services. | |

1-9-19.

Commanding, 5/6th Battalion The Royal Scots.
Captain,

Army Form C. 2118.

# WAR DIARY

## ~~INTELLIGENCE SUMMARY~~

(Erase heading not required.)   5/6TH. BN. THE ROYAL SCOTS. LOWLAND DIVISION.

Instructions regarding War Diaries and Intelligence
Summaries are contained in F. S. Regs., Part II.
and the Staff Manual respectively. Title pages
will be prepared in manuscript.

| Place | Date | Hour | Summary of Events and Information | Remarks and references to Appendices |
|---|---|---|---|---|
| Duren. | 1919. Sept. 1. | | "A" & "D" Coys. Education. "B" & "C" Coys. Company Training, P.T. & Ceremonial. | |
| | 2. | | "B" & "C" Coys. Company Training, P.T. and Ceremonial Drill. "A" & "D" Coys. Education. | |
| | 3. | | "A" & "D" Coys. Training. "B" & "C" Coys Education. "D" Coy. Range Practices. "The Dorris Cloud" Concert Party gave a Concert in the Theatre at 18.30 hours. | |
| | 4. | | "A" & "D" Coys. Education. "B" & "C" Coys. Company Training. | |
| | 5. | | Battalion Route March. Parade on Square at 09.00 hours. | |
| | 6. | | Coys. at disposal of Company Commanders. Inter-Coy. Shoot. "A" Coy. won. | |
| | 7. | | Divine Service. | |
| | 8. | | Holiday. 4th Corps Sports on Germania Sportsplatz. 5/6th Bn. represented the Brigade. | |
| | 9. | | "A" & "D" Coys. Education. "B" & "C" Coys. Company Training. | |
| | 10. | | "D" Coy. Range Practices. "A" Coy. Bayonet Training. "B" & "C" Coys. Education. The Battalion has been chosen to represent the 4th Corps in the British Army of the Rhine Athletic Meeting on 17th & 18th September. | |
| | 11. | | Active Service Army Schools Examination for 2nd Class Certificate, also notification of grant of Victory Medal. | |
| | 12. | | Active Service Army Schools Examination for 3rd Class Certificate. Nightly Cinema Performance in Barrack Theatre at 18.30 hours commences from this day. | |
| | 13. | | "A" & "B" Coys. Commanding Officer inspects kits. "C" & "D" Inter-Coy. Shoot result "D" 122 points, "C" Coy. 101 points. | |

Army Form C. 2118.

# WAR DIARY
## ~~INTELLIGENCE SUMMARY~~

(Erase heading not required.)

5/6TH. BN. THE ROYAL SCOTS. LOWLAND DIVISION.

| Place | Date | Hour | Summary of Events and Information | Remarks and references to Appendices |
|---|---|---|---|---|
| Düren. | 1919. Sept. 14. | | Divine Services. Battalion Boxing Competition at 14.00 hours in Theatre. | |
| | 15. | | "A" & "D" Coys Examination. "B" & "C" Coys. Route March. | |
| | 16. | | "A" & "D" Coys. Route March. "B" & "C" Coys. Examination. | |
| | 17. | | Rhine Army Sports, RIEHL, KÖLN. 1st day. | |
| | 18. | | do. do. 2nd day. Battalion Parades at 07.00 hours and proceeds to Sports by train. | |
| | 19. | | "A" & "D" Coys. Education. "B" & "C" Coys. Cleaning Barracks. | |
| | 20. | | "B" & "C" Coys. Education. "A" & "D" Coys. cleaning Barracks. The "Cheerios" Battalion Concert Party gave a performance in Barrack Theatre at 18.30 hours. | |
| | 21. | | Divine Services. | |
| | 22. | | "A" & "D" Coys. Education. "B" & "C" Coys Company Training and Ceremonial Drill. | |
| | 23. | | "B" & "C" Coys. Education. "A" Coy. Company Training. | |
| | 24. | | "A" & "D" Coys. Education. "B" & "C" Coys. Company Training and Musketry. "B" & "C" Inter-Company shoot. Result "C" Coy. 117 points, "B" Coy. 77 points. | |
| | 25. | | "B" & "C" Coys. Education. "A" & "D" Coys. Company Training. | |
| | 26. | | All Coys. Education. | |
| | 27. | | All Coys. Range Practices and cleaning Barracks. Leave to U.K. stopped owing to Railway trouble in England. | |
| | 28. | | Divine Services. | |

Army Form C. 2118.

# WAR DIARY
## or
## INTELLIGENCE SUMMARY.

5/6TH. BN. THE ROYAL SCOTS. LOWLAND DIVISION.

*(Erase heading not required.)*

Instructions regarding War Diaries and Intelligence Summaries are contained in F. S. Regs., Part II. and the Staff Manual respectively. Title pages will be prepared in manuscript.

| Place | Date | Hour | Summary of Events and Information | Remarks and references to Appendices |
|---|---|---|---|---|
| Duren. | 1919. Sept. 29. | | "A" Coy. Education. "B" & "C" Coys Company Training. Performance by Lowland Divisional Cinema in the Theatre. | |
| | 30. | | "B" & "C" Coys. Education. The Officers, N.C.Os. and men of "D" Coy. are posted to the remaining three Coys. "D" Coy. ceases to exist. | |

Lieut.-Col.,
Commanding, 5/6th Bn. The Royal Scots.

5/4th Bn. The Royal S[u]ss[e]x WAR DIARY for month of October Army Form C. 2118.

## INTELLIGENCE SUMMARY.
(Erase heading not required.)

| Place | Date | Hour | Summary of Events and Information | Remarks and references to Appendices |
|---|---|---|---|---|
| DÜREN | 1 | | All Coys are employed on every morning D by having been attached to A and C Coys. Cpl. J.J. Robertson is attached to B. Who has a gift in German. Education and Coy. Training. | |
| | 2 | | Route March. | |
| | 3 | | A. R. Amusements Committee is formed to arrange amusements for the men during the coming winter. | |
| | 4 | | Range Parties and Cleaning Billets. | |
| | 5 | | Divine Service in Theatre. Hindenburg Barracks. | |
| | 6-10 | | All Coys on Education and Games. | |
| | 11 | | A and C Coys. Cleaning Barracks and Range Practices. B. Coy. taken over Town Piquet from 11th Royal Scots at Peppeh St. School, Quick Taster. | |
| | 12 | | Divine Service in Coy. Training. | |
| | 13.14 | | Education and Coy. Training | |
| | 15 | | Route March. | |
| | 16 | | Education and Training for Relieving Cavalry Pickets. "Shields" Brigade to Brigade Army by Corps Magazine. | |

7th Bn The Royal Scots

WAR DIARY for month of October

INTELLIGENCE SUMMARY.
(Erase heading not required)

Army Form C. 2118.

Instructions regarding War Diaries and Intelligence Summaries are contained in F. S. Regs., Part II and the Staff Manual respectively. Title pages will be prepared in manuscript.

| Place | Date | Hour | Summary of Events and Information | Remarks and references to Appendices |
|---|---|---|---|---|
| DOREN | 17. | | Education. | |
| | 18. | | Cleaning Billets, Kit Inspection and Economical Drills. | |
| | 19. | | 10 Coys returned from Town Piquet. Rumour service in Meston. | |
| | 20-21 | | Education, Coy training and Range Practices. | |
| | 22. | | Coys at Musketry and Coy Commanders. | |
| | 23-24. | | Education and Coy training. | |
| | 25. | | Bn is ordered to Cadre, and all the Officers A.C.O's and men are transferred to 1/4 Bn The Royal Scots. | |
| | 26-31 | | Return and packing of equipment home to Embarkation. | |

D MacCapt.
O/C 1/7th Bn The Royal Scots

www.ingramcontent.com/pod-product-compliance
Lightning Source LLC
Chambersburg PA
CBHW081508160426
43193CB00014B/2617